CONTENTS

W9-BZC-174

FRENCH ONION SOUP

Metric	Ingredient	Imperial
	(for the soup)	
	4 large onions	
1 litre	beef stock (use homemade onion stock to make a vegetarian soup)	2 pints
	1 tbsp flour	
	butter	
	(for the croutons)	
	4 slices bread	
	1 clove garlic	
	1 tbsp olive oil	
	butter	

Method
The soup:

1. **Slice the onions into** rings and sauté them gently in the butter (don't use olive oil for this). Don't rush this, let the onions brown very gently. If some brown bits appear on the bottom of your pan, don't worry, these are the sugars from the onions that have caramelized. They'll dissolve when you add the stock.

2. **Add the flour and** stir. The flour will seem to have disappeared, but has been absorbed into the butter. This will give the soup its characteristic slight thickness.

3. **Add a quarter of** the stock and stir for a while. Add another quarter of the stock and keep stirring. Repeat for the remaining stock.

The croutons:

1. **Crush and chop the** garlic. Put the olive oil and butter into the pan and lightly sauté the garlic.

2. **Increase the heat a** little and fry the slices of bread until golden.

3. **Serve the soup with** the croutons floating in it.

FRESH BORSCHT

Metric	Ingredient	Imperial
	3 thinly sliced small potatoes	
128 g	thinly sliced beets.	1 cup
950 ml	water	4 cups
15 g	butter	1 tbsp
192 g	chopped onion	1½ cups
7.5 g	salt	1½ tsp
	1 stalk celery, chopped	
	1 medium carrot, chopped	
690 g	shredded cabbage	3 cups
	a little fresh ground black pepper	
5 g	dill weed	1 tsp
30 ml	cider vinegar	2 tbsp
5 g	brown sugar or honey	1 tbsp
230 g	tomato purée	1 cup

Method

1. **Place the potatoes, beets,** and water in a medium-sized saucepan. Cover and cook over medium heat until tender (20-30 minutes). While that is cooking, do steps 2-3.

2. **Melt the butter in** a Dutch oven/soup pot. Add the onion and salt. Cook over medium heat, stirring occasionally, until the onions are translucent (8 to 10 minutes).

3. **Add the celery, carrots,** cabbage, and two cups of the water in which the potatoes and beets are cooking. Cover and cook over medium heat until the vegetables are tender (8 to 10 minutes).

4. **Add the remaining soup** ingredients (including the potatoes, beets, and the rest of the water in which they are cooking). Cover and simmer for at least 15 more minutes. Correct the seasonings. If it is too thin, let it simmer uncovered, and maybe add a little more tomato paste.

5. **Serve hot, topped with** sour cream or yoghurt and sprinkled with dill. (If desired the sour cream or yoghurt can be served with the soup and used as a condiment to taste.)

OXTAIL SOUP

Metric	Ingredient	Imperial
	Half an Oxtail (the thin end)	
	1 Onion	
	1 Carrot	
	1 Small Turnip	
	1 Celery Stick	
	Small Bunch of Herbs	
	6 Peppercorns	
	2 Cloves	
	Piece of Mace	
25g	Butter	1 oz
1.8 litres	Beef Stock or Water	3 pints
15 g	Plain Flour	1 tbsp
	Salt & Pepper	

Method

1. **First joint the oxtail** and blanch it (put it into a saucepan with a pinch of salt, cover with cold water and bring to the boil. Strain off the water, put the joints into cold water for a minute, then wipe them with a cloth).

2. **Season a dessertspoon of** flour with salt & pepper, and roll the joints of oxtail in it. Melt the butter in a saucepan, and brown the joints well in this, turning them over so that both sides are browned. Add the stock or water and bring to the boil. Let it boil gently for half an hour, removing the scum as it rises.

3. **Prepare the vegetables and** cut them into quarters and add, together with the herbs and spices tied in a piece of muslin. Season with salt & pepper an simmer for three and a half hours. Then strain off the stock.

4. **Reserve the pieces of** oxtail, rub the vegetables through a sieve (or blend), skim off any fat from the stock, add the vegetable puree to it. Put them in a saucepan, mix the remainder of the flour with a little stock. When the soup is hot, add the flour and stir while it boils gently for five minutes. Add the pieces of the meat and serve hot.

TOM YAM KUNG

Metric	Ingredient	Imperial
200 g	mushrooms	1 cup
	2 spring onions	
	16 peeled prawns	
1 litre	chicken soup stock	4 cups
45 ml	lemon juice	3 tbsp
5 g	chili paste	1 tsp
45 ml	fish sauce	3 tbsp
	1/2 Kaffir-lime	

Method

1. **In a pot, bring** the chicken soup stock to boil.

2. **Cut the mushrooms in** half.

3. **Cut the spring onions** into 2 cm long pieces.

3. **Add the lemon juice,** chili paste and fish sauce to the chicken soup stock and stir in.

4. **Add mushrooms, spring onions** and prawns and let simmer for ten minutes.

5. **Reduce heat and season** with Kaffir-lime juice.

VEGETABLE SOUP

Metric	Ingredient	Imperial
15 ml	olive oil	1 tbsp
14 g	unsalted butter	1 tbsp
	1 sized onion	
	2 carrots	
	1 handful green beans	
	8 button mushrooms	
1 litre	chicken stock	4 cups
750 ml	water	3 cups
	6 potatos	
	salt and pepper	
60 g	parsley	1/4 cup

Method

1. Heat the butter and oil on medium to high heat in a soup pot.

2. Sauté the onion, carrot, and green beans for 3-4 minutes.

3. Add the mushrooms and cook for another 2 minutes. Add the chicken stock, water, potatoes

4. Season with salt & pepper.

5. Bring to the boil, then cover and reduce the heat. Cook at a gentle boil until the potatoes are tender. (which should be around 15 minutes). Add parsley just before the potatoes are cooked.

6. Season to taste and serve.

BAKED BEEF STEW

Metric	Ingredient	Imperial
900g	beef	2 lbs
1.36 litre	tomato juice (one large can)	46 fl. oz
298 g	double-strength beef broth	10 1/2 oz
115 g	flour	1/2 cup
62 ml	oil	1/4 cup
	1 bay leaf	
5ml	marjoram	1 tsp
5ml	oregano	1 tsp
	2 to 4 russet (large non-sweet white baking) potatoes	
	4 large carrots	
	4 stalks of celery	

Method

1. Cut the beef into chunks about 1" (2.5cm) in diameter.

2. Put the beef and flour in a container, such as a plastic bag, and shake or squish until the beef is well-coated. Use more flour for a thicker stew, or less for a thinner stew.

3. Put oil into a wide pot and heat it.

4. In several batches, brown the beef in the pot with the oil.

5. Into the pot: the beef, spices, tomato juice, and the double-strength beef broth (w/o water).

6. Cover the pot, then simmer for at least an hour to soften the beef. Stir the stew every few minutes to prevent the beef from burning on the bottom of the pot.

7. Peel the carrots, cut them into pieces about the same size as the beef, add them to the stew, and simmer a bit more. (stirring every few minutes)

8. Cut the other vegetables likewise, and simmer a bit more. (stirring every few minutes)

9. When all the vegetables are soft but not yet falling apart, remove the bay leaf and serve the stew.

BAKED JUICY PORK TENDERLOIN

Metric	Ingredient	Imperial
	1 medium onion, finely chopped	1
30 ml	olive or canola oil	2 tbsp
15 ml	lemon juice	1 tbsp
5 g	minced fresh rosemary	1 tsp
5 g	minced fresh thyme	1 tsp
5 g	grated lemon peel	1 tsp
	1 garlic clove, minced	
2 g	rock salt	½ tsp
2 g	pepper	½ tsp
	2 pork tenderloins	

Method

1. Combine the onion, oil, lemon juice, herbs, lemon peel in a bowl and mix together.

2. Rub the mixture over the tenderloins and add the rock salt and pepper.

3. Place the tenderloins on a rack in a shallow roasting pan.

4. Bake uncovered at 400°F or until a meat thermometer reads 160°F.

5. Cover with foil and let stand 10 minutes before slicing.

BAVARIAN ROASTED KNUCKLE OF PORK

Metric	Ingredient	Imperial
	4 Fresh Pork knuckles (Not pickled or salted)	
	Rock Salt	
	1 Large Onion	
500ml	gravy mix	2 cups

Method

1. **Preheat the oven to** 200/220.

2. **Slash the fat (skin)** on the pork at 1 inch intervals (or you could ask your butcher to do this for you.)

3. **Rub the rock salt** into the the skin and slits of the pork.

4. **Place Knuckles into a** roasting tin with 1 or 2 cups of water and place into the oven for a total of 3 hours.

5. **After 1/2 hour turn** knuckles and then again every 1/2 hour; making sure that the water does not boil off, replenishing as necessary.

7. **After 2 1/2 hours,** cut the onion into 6 wedges and place into the roasting tin and leave to cook for the last 1/2 hour.

8. **Remove the pork from** the oven and allow it to stand for 10 to 15 minutes.

9. **Place the liquid from** the bottom of the roasting tin in a separator and remove the fat. Make up the gravy and add the remaining liquid to the mix. Place the onion pieces into the gravy and then pour over the pork.

10. **Traditionaly served with boiled** cabbage.

BEEF RAGOUT HOT POT

Metric	Ingredient	Imperial
	4-6 potatoes, sliced	
	2 large carrots, sliced	
2 g	parsley (to garnish)	1/2 tsp
450 g	beef stew meat (cut chunks into halves)	1 lb
	1 onion, sliced	
300 ml	beef stock	1 1/2 cups
30 g	butter, melted & divided	2 tbsps

Method

1. Preheat oven to 375°F.

2. Heat a little oil in frying pan & brown the beef along with the onions & the carrots; remove this from the pan.

3. Layer the sliced potatoes, carrots & meat into a 3 pint casserole dish, onion, finishing with a layer of potatoes.

4. Pour over the stock.

5. Brush the potatoes with 1 tbsp melted butter.

6. Cover up & bake for 1 hr.

7. Remove the hot pot from the oven.

8. Uncover & brush the potatoes again with melted butter or dripping.

9. Return to the oven for a further 30 mins, uncovered, to brown the potatoes.

10. Serve garnished with parsley.

BEEF STEW WITH SUET DUMPLINGS

Metric	Ingredient	Imperial
	(For the stew)	
680 g	lean cubed beef	1 1/2 pound
15 ml	Tablespoon of cooking oil	1 tbsp
	1 large onion, sliced	
	3 large carrots, in chunks	
	1 large raw potato cut into large cubes	
900 ml	beef stock	2 pints
15 g	plain flour	3 tsp
	(For the dumplings)	
225 g	plain flour	8 oz
115 g	shredded beef suet	4 oz
2 g	salt	1/2 tsp
5 g	baking powder	1 tsp
	Water	

Method

1. **In a large, lidded** saucepan or casserole, fry the beef in the oil until well browned. Don't worry if it sticks a little - the browning is important. Add the onions and gently fry for five minutes. Add the flour and stir in well. Add the carrots and potato to warm through, then add the stock, stir well until the sauce thickens and boils. Cover and simmer gently for 25 minutes Meanwhile, make the dumplings. Stir the shredded suet through the flour, salt and baking powder. Begin adding water while stirring until you have a soft but moldable dough.

2. **After the stew has** cooked 25 minutes, stir it through then add the dumplings as balls about 2 inches diameter, to rest on top of the stew. Cover and either continue to simmer on the hob for 20 minutes, or place in an oven, uncovered, at 175C for 20 minutes.

3. **The stew can also** include turnip or swede instead of potato, and the dumplings can include plenty of herbs - great with dried sage, thyme or parsley.

BEEF STROGANOFF

Metric	Ingredient	Imperial
450g	beef chuck roast	1 pound
2 g	salt	1/2 tsp
2 g	ground black pepper	1/2 tsp
110g	butter	4 ounces
	4 green onions, sliced (white parts only)	
20 g	all-purpose flour	4 tsp
300g	can condensed beef broth	10.5 ounce
5 g	prepared mustard	1 tsp
150g	can sliced mushrooms, drained	6 ounce
160ml	sour cream	1/3 cup
160ml	white wine	1/3 cup

Method

1. **Remove any fat and** gristle from the roast and cut into strips 1/2 inch thick by 2 inches long. Season with 1/2 teaspoon of both salt and pepper.

2. **In a large skillet** over a medium heat, melt the butter and brown the beef strips quickly, then push the beef strips off to one side. Add the onions and cook slowly for 3 to 5 minutes, then push to the side with the beef strips.

3. **Stir the flour into** the juices on the empty side of the pan. Pour in beef broth and bring to a boil, stirring constantly. Lower the heat and stir in the mustard.

4. **Cover and simmer for** 1 hour or until the meat is tender.

5. **Five minutes before serving,** stir in the mushrooms, sour cream, and white wine. Heat briefly then salt and pepper to taste.

BLACK TRUFFLED POUSSINS

Metric	Ingredient	Imperial
	2 boned out poussins (also called a spring chicken)	
30 g	black truffles, sliced very thin	1 oz
30 ml	oil	2 tbsp

Method

1. **Slide the truffles in** between the skin and breast meat of the poussin

2. **Keep covered in the** refrigerator for a day

3. **In a large sauté** pan heat the oil until hot

4. **Salt and pepper the** poussin on both sides

5. **Place poussin skin side** down in the pan and cook on high heat until golden brown

6. **Reduce heat to medium** and continue to cook on skin-side only until completely cooked, approximately 6 minutes

7. **Flip birds over and** cook on flesh side for thirty seconds

8. **Serve immediately**

BOEUF BOURGIGNON

Metric	Ingredient	Imperial
1.8 kg	beef shoulder (stewing beef) cut into 2 inch cubes	4 lbs
170 g	bacon	6 oz
	4 carrots, peeled and sliced	
	1 large onion, chopped	
450 g	mushrooms, sliced	1 lb
	2 stalks celery, chopped	
	1 bottle red burgundy wine (young wine)	
500 ml	beef bouillon (beef stock)	2 cups
28 g	flour	1oz
	olive oil	
	butter	1oz
	1 small bunch parsley	
	1 sprig thyme	
	1 clove garlic, mashed	
	18 small white onions	

Method

1. Cut the bacon into small strips then simmer for 10 minutes in water. Dry the bacon and then cook in a large heavy-bottomed saucepan with the olive oil at moderate heat for 2 or 3 minutes. Remove bacon.

3. Using the same saucepan, cook the beef in the bacon's fat until browned. Remove the beef. Still in the same pan, put the onion, carrots, celery and cook for 2 or 3 minutes. Remove the saucepan from the heat. Remove the fat from the saucepan.

5. Mix the butter and the flour to make a paste.

6. Put the beef and bacon with the vegetables back into the pan. Add salt and pepper. Cover the beef cubes with the butter and flour mixture. Cook for 3 or 4 minutes, uncovered, and turn the beef cubes.

7. Pour in the wine and enough bouillon so that it covers the ingredients. Add small white onions, garlic and herbs. Bring to a boil. Cover the pan and simmer for 3 hours on a low heat.

9. Saute mushrooms in butter. Add mushrooms to Boeuf Bourguignon. Garnish with parsley.

BOUILLABAISSE

Metric	Ingredient	Imperial	Metric	Ingredient	Imperial
	(For the broth)		250 ml	of olive oil	1 cup
660 g	sea robin, sliced	1 1/2 lb		1 bouquet garni	
660 g	scorpionfish, sliced	1 1/2 lb		1 branch of fennel	
660 g	red gurnard, sliced	1 1/2 lb		8 threads of saffron	
660 g	conger, sliced	1 1/2 lb		10 slices of country bread	
660 g	lotte, or monkfish, sliced	1 1/2 lb		salt and cayenne pepper	
660 g	John Dory, sliced	1 1/2 lb		(For the rouille)	
	10 sea urchins			1 egg yolk	
1 kg	potato	2 lb		2 cloves of garlic	
	7 cloves of garlic		250 ml	olive oil	1 cup
	3 onions, sliced			10 threads of saffron	
	5 tomatoes, peeled, quartered and without seeds			salt and cayenne pepper	

Method

1. **Warm the olive oil** in a large, deep saucepan. Add the onions, along with six cloves of crushed garlic, the octopus pieces and tomatoes. Brown at low heat turning gently for five minutes.

2. **Add the fish slices;** first the large slices then the smaller ones. Cover with boiling water and add salt, pepper, fennel, the bouquet garni and saffron. Simmer while stirring, so the fish doesn't stick to the pan. Remove the bouillabaise from the heat once the oil and water have thoroughly blended with the other ingredients.

3. **Use a mortar to** crush the garlic cloves into a fine paste after removing the stems. Add the egg yolk and the saffron, then blend in the olive oil little by little to make a mayonnaise, stirring it with the pounder of the mortar.

4. **Cook the potatoes, peeled** and boiled and cut into large slices, in salted water for 15 to 20 minutes. Open the sea urchins with a pair of scissors and remove the roe with a small spoon.

5. **Arrange the fish on** a platter. Add the sea urchin roe into the broth and stir.

6. **Rub several slices of** bread with garlic and spread a tablespoon of rouille on each. Place at least two slices per serving bowl.

7. **Remove the fish and** potatoes from the broth and place them on a large serving platter. Pour the hot broth in each bowl containing a slice of bread smothered in rouille. Then serve the fish and the potatoes on a separate platter

BRAISED SHIN OF BEEF

Metric	Ingredient	Imperial
30 ml	olive oil	2 tbsp
500g	un-smoked pancetta, chopped into large cubes	1lb 2oz
1.5kg	shin of beef, sliced into 2.5cm (1in) wide rounds	3lb 5oz
85ml	red wine	3fl oz
1kg	large organic winter carrots, peeled and roughly chopped	2¼lb
	1 head of celery, roughly chopped	
1kg	pickling onions or shallots	2¼lb
1kg	tomatoes, roasted and sieved to a purée	2¼lb
1 litre	good beef stock or water	1¾ pints
	1 bouquet garni	
	1 Large Swede	
250g	Brocolli	9oz

Method

1. **Heat the oil in** a large, heavy-bottomed frying pan. Add the pancetta and fry until brown and crispy. Remove from the pan and add to a large stock pot or casserole dish.

2. **Fry the shin of** beef in the frying pan, on both sides, until well browned. Transfer the shin to the stock pot.

3. **Pour the red wine** into the frying pan and stir, for 2-3 minutes to collect the cooking juices. Tip into the pot.

4. **Place the stock pot** over a gentle heat. Add the carrots, celery and onions. Pour in the tomato purée and enough stock or water to cover the meat and vegetables. Add the bouquet garni and cover with a lid.

5. **Simmer for 3-4 hours,** stirring occasionally.

6. **Cut off the outer** skin of the swede. Dice the swede into small cubes and boil in water until soft. Season with salt and pepper. Serve with the boiled brocolli (according to prefered texture).

BRAZILIAN SHRIMP STEW

Metric	Ingredient	Imperial
1.2kg	medium size shrimp, peeled and de-veined	3 lbs
1.2kg	yuca root (cassava, manioc)	3 lb
460 g	onion, chopped	2 cups
	3 cloves garlic, chopped	
125 ml	olive oil	½ cup
	6 medium tomatoes, peeled and seeded	
60 ml	cilantro, chopped	¼ cup
500 ml	· coconut milk	2 cups
60 ml	palm oil (also known as dendê)	¼ cup

Method

1. **Peel and cut the** manioc and put in a pan with cold water and salt. Cook until tender, drain and reserve both the cooked manioc and the liquid. Discard any manioc fiber.

2. **Using a fork, mash** the manioc while still hot. Use some of the liquid to help in the process. Do not use a blender or food processor.

4. **Sauté the onion and** garlic in the olive oil until wilted.

5. **Add 1/2 of the** chopped cilantro and the tomatoes, stirring well then add the shrimp and cook it for around 15 minutes. Add the puréed manioc.

6. **Check the amount of** liquid and add more of the reserved manioc liquid to thin the mixture, if necessary. Add the coconut milk, the remaining cilantro and the palm oil.

Serve over Brazilian white rice.

CALVES LIVER AND BACON

Metric	Ingredient	Imperial
	4 pieces of calves liver	
	2 large onions, sliced	
	olive oil	
225 g	bacon, diced	1/2 lb
115 g	flour	1/2 cup

Method

1. **In a large skillet,** cook the bacon until crisp. Then remove the bacon, and set aside.

2. **Mix the flour with** some salt and pepper.

3. **Place the flour mixture** on a large plate and dredge the liver.

4. **Place in a fridge** until ready to cook.

5. **Take half of the** bacon drippings and add to another large skillet. Bring the heat to medium and add onions and cook until tender.

6. **In another skillet, heat** the bacon drippings on a medium to high heat then add calves liver and cook a minute or 2 on each side.

7. **Serve and top with** onions and bacon bits.

CARIBBEAN STYLE CURRIED OXTAIL STEW

Metric	Ingredient	Imperial
1¼ kgs	oxtail	
20 g	cornflour	4 tsps
30 g	vegetable oil	2 tbsps
14 g	salt	1 tbsp
30 g	black pepper	2 tbsps
	4 rashers bacon	
	2 medium onion	
	1 garlic clove	
	4 medium carrots	
230 g	tomatoes (chopped)	1 cup
½ litre	hot water	2 cups
	2 stalks escallion	
	1 sprig thyme	
	2 cans butter beans	

Method

1. **Cut the oxtail into** bite-size pieces. Slice the onions and carrots, crush the garlic, chop the tomatoes and finely slice the escallion. Trim away any excess fat and place the oxtail pieces into boiling water for 2-3 minutes. Dry well on absorbent paper and coat with corn flour.

2. **Sprinkle with salt and** pepper.

3. **Heat the oil in** a heavy bottom pot and brown each piece of the oxtail on both sides, removing them when browned. Pour off any excess oil.

4. **Dice the bacon and** fry for a few minutes, then return the oxtail to the pot with bacon along with the carrots, onion, garlic, tomatoes and hot water.

5. **Cover and simmer gently** for 3 hours or until the oxtail is almost tender. Add more liquid if necessary and season to taste.

6. **Cover and simmer for** a final 20-30 minutes. Add the butter beans and allow them to simmer for 3 minutes.

COCK A LEEKIE

Metric	Ingredient	Imperial
	1 boiling fowl, about 4lb, including legs and wings	
450 g	leeks (about 12) cleaned and cut into 1-inch pieces	1 lb
1.8 litres	stock or water	4 pints
30 g	long grained rice	1oz
115 g	cooked, stoned prunes	4oz
5 g	brown sugar	1 tsp
	Salt and pepper	
	Garni of bay leaf, parsley, thyme	
	3 chopped rashers of streaky bacon	

Method

1. **Put the fowl and** bacon in a large saucepan and cover with water.

2. **Bring to the boil** and remove any scum. Add three-quarters of the leeks, (green as well as white sections), herbs (tied together in a bundle), salt and pepper and return to the boil. Simmer gently for 2-3 hours, adding more water if necessary.

3. **Remove the bird and** cut the meat into small pieces and add them back to the soup. Add the rice, drained prunes and the remaining leeks and simmer for another 30 minutes. Check for flavour and serve with a little chopped parsley.

CONFIT DUCK LEGS

Metric	Ingredient	Imperial
	4 duck leg portions with thighs attached, excess fat trimmed and reserved	
14 g	salt	1 tbsp
2 g	freshly ground black pepper	½ tsp
	10 garlic cloves	
	4 bay leaves	
	4 sprigs fresh thyme	
7 g	black peppercorns	1½ tsp
2 g	table salt	½ tsp
500 ml	olive oil	2 cups

Method

1. **Lay the leg portions** on a platter, skin side down and sprinkle with the kosher salt and the black pepper. Place the garlic cloves, bay leaves, and sprigs of thyme on each of 2 leg portions.

2. **Lay the remaining 2** leg portions, flesh to flesh, on top. Put the fat from the ducks in the bottom of a glass or plastic container. Top with the sandwiched leg portions. Cover and refrigerate for 12 hours.

3. **Preheat the oven to** 200°F (95°C). Remove the duck from the refrigerator.

4. **Remove the garlic, bay** leaves, thyme, and duck fat and set asside. Rinse the duck with cool water, rubbing off some of the salt and pepper. Pat dry with paper towels.

5. **Put the garlic, bay** leaves, thyme, and duck fat in the bottom of an enamelled cast iron pot. Sprinkle evenly with the peppercorns and table salt.

6. **Lay the duck on** top, skin side down. Add the olive oil. Cover and bake for 12 to 14 hours, or until the meat pulls away from the bone.

7. **Remove the duck from** the fat. Strain the fat and set asside.

COQ AU VIN

Metric	Ingredient	Imperial
1.5 kg	chicken, cut up	3 lb
	1 onion, diced	
	1 carrot, chopped	
40 g	flour	3 tbsp
2 g	salt	1/2 tsp
1 g	pepper	1/4 tsp
200 g	small mushrooms	1/2 lb
240 ml	red wine	1 cup
	1 clove garlic, minced	
5 g	basil, chopped and fresh	1 tsp
5 g	fresh or dried Thyme	1 tsp
	Olive oil for sauteing	

Method

1. Mix the flour, salt and pepper, then coat the chicken, onion and the carrot in the flour mixture and set aside.

2. Sauté the mushrooms, and then set aside.

3. Brown the chicken pieces a few at a time, and then set aside.

4. Brown the onions and the carrots. Put the chicken into a large casserole dish on a medium-high heat along with the onions, carrots and mushrooms.

5. Combine the wine, garlic, and the basil; pour over chicken. Cover the casserole, then cook until the chicken is ready (1-1.5 hours), stirring occasionally.

CULLEN SKINK

Metric	Ingredient	Imperial
	1 large smoked haddock of around	
	1 medium onion, chopped fine.	
900ml	milk	1 1/2 pints
30 g	butter	2 tbsp
230 g	mashed potato	8 oz
	Salt and pepper	
	1 bay leaf	
	Chopped parsley	
	Water	

Method

1. Cover the haddock with water in a shallow pan with the skin side down. Bring to the boil and then simmer for 5 minutes turning once.

2. Take the fish from the pan and remove the skin and bones. Flake the fish and return to the stock.

3. Add the chopped onion, bay leaf, salt and pepper then simmer for a further 10 minutes.

4. Strain off the stock and keep it ready - discard the bay leaf and keep the fish warm.

5. Add the milk to the fish stock and bring to the boil then add the mashed potato to make a rich and thick soup.

6. Add the fish and check the seasoning - add more if needed. When serving, add the butter in small pieces so it runs through the soup. Serve with chopped parsley on top, and toast by the side.

FILLETS OF PORK IN A CREAM SAUCE

Metric	Ingredient	Imperial
675 g	pork fillet	1 1/2 lb
15 g	flour	1 tbsp
	salt and freshly ground pepper	
25 g	butter	1 oz
30 ml	oil	2 tbsp
	1 onion, peeled and finely chopped	
250 g	Herbed Rice	8 oz
30 ml	brandy	2 tbsp
	pinch nutmeg	
150 ml	single cream	1/4 pt
	4 lemon wedges	
	a bunch of watercress	

Method

1. **Trim the pork fillets.** Remove any gristle and excess fat. Cut into diagonal slices. Beat out to about 1 cm (1/2 in) thick.

2. **Mix the flour with** the seasoning and coat each slice evenly.

3. **Heat the butter and** oil in a frying pan and cook the onions for 4 minutes. Remove onto a plate with a slotted spoon.

5. **Prepare and cook the** Herbed Rice.

6. **On a medium heat** saute the pork fillet slices for about 4 minutes each side until golden brown. Heat the brandy in a ladle and set alight. Pour onto the pork and allow to flambe.

7. **Serve the Herbed Rice** on a warmed serving dish. Arrange the pork slices on top and keep warm in a low oven.

8. **Add nutmeg and single** cream to the frying pan and stir over a low heat to combine the meat juices and cream.

9. **Pour the sauce over** the meat. Garnish with the lemon wedges and watercress and accompany with a crisp green salad.

GOOSE BAKED WITH POTATOES AND ONIONS

Metric	Ingredient	Imperial
	1/2 head of cabbage, cut up	
	1 Large onion	
	3 lg. potatoes, sliced	
	1/2 to 1 roll of smoked sausage or kielbasa, sliced	
	1 can cream of mushroom soup	
	1/2 soup can of water	
	Shredded cheese (opt.)	
	Salt & pepper to taste	

Method

1. In a 1 1/2 quart casserole place cut up cabbage and onion, then place the potatoes on top of cabbage.

2. Arrange slices of the sausage on top of potatoes. Pour the mushroom soup over this, then pour water over all.

3. Put in 350 degree oven. After 20 minutes, stir well. Continue baking until potatoes and cabbage are tender. If cheese is used, put it on approximately 5 minutes before finishing baking.

HAGGIS NEEPS AND TATTIES

Metric	Ingredient	Imperial	Metric	Ingredient	Imperial
450 g	beef heart, cut into 2-inch-wide strips	1 pound	10 g	salt	2 tsp
			2 g	freshly ground black pepper	1/2 tsp
450 g	beef liver	1 pound	5 g	dried thyme, whole	1 tsp
225 g	lamb stew meat, cut in 1-inch cubes	1/2 pound	2 g	dried rosemary	1/2 tsp
			1 g	freshly grated nutmeg	1/4 tsp
375 g	peeled and finely chopped yellow onion	1 1/2 cups		(For the casing)	
				3 beef CAPS	
60 ml	Scotch whisky	4 tbsp	250 ml	distilled white vinegar	1 cup
15 ml	Egg nog	1 tbsp	7 g	salt for soaking	1/2 tbsp
460 g	oatmeal, toasted	2 cups			

Method

1. **Place the beef heart** in a 4-quart covered pot and just cover with cold water. Simmer, covered, for 1 hour and 10 minutes.

2. **Add the beef liver** and lamb stew meat, and cover and simmer for 20 minutes. Remove the contents of the pot and cool. Reserve 1 cup of the liquid. Grind everything coarsely.

3. **In a large bowl** mix all of the ingredients, except for the beef caps, vinegar, and salt for soaking. Mix well and set aside.

4. **Rinse the beef caps** in cold water. Turn them inside out and soak them in 2 quarts of cold water with the salt and vinegar for 1/2 hour. Drain them and rinse very well, inside and out.

5. **Divide the meat mixture** into three parts. Fill the beef caps with the meat mixture and tie the ends off with string. Two will have to be tied on just one end, but the third piece will be tied on both ends. Prick the Haggis all over with corn holders or a sharp fork. Place in a steamer and steam for 1 hour and 20 minutes.
Serve the Haggis, sliced, with beef or lamb gravy.

HAM AND VEGETABLE STEW

Metric	Ingredient	Imperial
1 litre	water	4 cups
	2 cans diced tomatoes, undrained	
690 g	shredded cabbage	3 cups
460 g	diced fully cooked lean ham	2 cups
	3 large carrots, cut into 1-inch pieces	
345 g	chopped celery	1 1/2 cups
170 g	chopped onion	3/4 cup
115 g	chopped green pepper	1/2 cup
14 g	sugar	1 tbsp
10 g	dried basil	2 tsp
2 g	pepper	1/2 tsp
1 g	garlic powder	1/4 tsp
	2 bay leaves	
60 g	cornstarch	1/4 cup
60 g	cold water	1/4 cup

Method

1. **In a Dutch oven** or soup kettle, combine the first 13 ingredients and then bring to a boil.

2. **Reduce heat; cover and** simmer for 1 hour or until cabbage is tender, stirring occasionally.

3. **Combine cornstarch and cold** water until smooth; stir into stew. Bring to a boil and then cook and stir for 2 minutes or until thickened. Discard bay leaves.

HONEY ROASTED HAM

Metric	Ingredient	Imperial
5 kg	1 ready-to-eat ham with the bone	12 lb
45 g	dijon mustard	3 tbsp
230 g	brown sugar	1 cup
125 ml	honey	1/2 cup
5 g	cinnamon	1 tsp
375 ml	apple juice	1 1/2 cup
	handful of cloves	

Method

1. **Using a sharp knife,** remove the layer of skin from ham, leaving a thin layer of fat to keep the meat juicy while baking.

2. **Score the surface of** the ham in a diamond pattern, without cutting into the meat.

3. **Place a whole clove** in the center of half of the diamonds. Brush the top of the ham with Dijon mustard and then place the ham in a roasting pan.

4. **Combine the sugar, honey** and cinnamon then heat over a low to medium temperature for about 2 minutes until the mixture is pourable, but not thin.

5. **Spread the mixture over** the ham. Pour the apple juice into bottom of roasting pan and roast at 325 degrees for 1 1/2 hours. Baste every half-hour using the juices in the pan.

IRISH STEW

Metric	Ingredient	Imperial
1.1kg	boned mutton	2½ lb
	4 large potatoes	
	2 large onions	
	3 or 4 medium carrots	
	sprig of parsley	
480ml	water	2 cups
	salt and pepper	

Method

1. **Cut the meat into** good size chunks. Peel the vegetables and slice thickly. Chop the parsley.

2. **Choose a pot with** a well-fitting lid and put in the ingredients in layers, starting and finishing with potatoes. Pour in the water and season to taste.

3. **Cover and put on** a very low heat for about 2 1/2 hours until the meat is tender and the potatoes have thickened the liquid.

LAMB SHORT RIBS WITH MINT JELLY

Metric	Ingredient	Imperial
240 ml	one jar mint jelly	8 oz
60 ml	fresh lemon juice (about 1 lemon)	1/4 cup
	seeds from 4 cardamom pods	
30 g	cold unsalted butter, cut into pieces	2 tbsp
60 g	fresh mint leaves, cut into very thin strips	1/4 cup
	4 8-ounce double lamb rib chops, 1 1/2 inches thick	
	3 large cloves garlic, peeled and halved lengthwise	
30 ml	olive oil	2 tbsp
	kosher salt and freshly cracked black pepper to taste	

Method

1. **Preheat the broiler, set** on high if you have a choice.

2. **In a medium sauté** pan, warm the jelly over a low heat until it liquefies. Stir in the lemon juice and cardamom, then raise the heat, bring to a simmer, and simmer until the sauce is reduced by half, about 10 minutes.

3. **Remove from the heat** and add the cold butter a little at a time, swirling the pan to blend it into the sauce. Stir in the mint leaves and set aside.

4. **As soon as the** sauce is done, cook the chops: Dry the chops with paper towels, rub them with the cut sides of the garlic cloves, brush with olive oil, and season with salt and pepper.

5. **Place them on the** rack of the broiler pan about 3 inches from the heat source and cook until well seared on the outside and done to your liking on the inside, 5 to 6 minutes per side for medium rare. Remove the chops from the broiler and allow to rest for 5 minutes.

4. **Serve the chops accompanied** by the sauce.

LAMB STEW

Metric	Ingredient	Imperial
450 g	boneless lamb, cut in 1-inch cubes	1 pound
45 g	flour	3 tbsp
30 g	oil	2 tbsp
	dry onion gravy mix	
3 g	salt	3/4 tsp
1 g	garlic powder	1/4 tsp
	dash pepper	
500 ml	cold water	2 cups
	4 medium potatoes, peeled, halved, and sliced about 1/2-inch thick	
345 g	frozen green beans	1 1/2 cups

Method

1. **Toss the lamb cubes** with flour and then brown in a large skillet with hot oil. Drain off any excess fat.

2. **In a separate bowl,** combine gravy mix, salt, garlic powder, pepper and cold water then whisk until smooth.

3. **Add the mixture to** the meat. Cook, stirring occasionally, until the mixture thickens and bubbles. Cover and simmer for 30 minutes.

4. **Add sliced potatoes and** beans. Return to boiling then reduce the heat, cover, and simmer lamb stew for 30 minutes more or until vegetables are tender.

LANCASHIRE HOT POT

Metric	Ingredient	Imperial
900g	neck of lamb	2 lb
	2 large potatoes	
	1 large or 2 small onion(s)	
	choice of mixed herbs	
500 ml	boiling water	2 cups

Method

1. Dice the lamb and set aside. Preheat oven to 325F / 170C / Gas Mark 3.

2. Slice the potatoes and dice the onions. Add a layer of the potatoes to the bottom of a casserole dish, and cover with a handful of the diced onion. Layer the diced lamb over the top of this, sprinkling with your choice of herbs. Repeat these layers until the dish is full. Top with a final layer of the potatoes.

3. Pour boiling water into the dish until filled - if more water is needed, continue to add until topped. Bake for at least one hour, though traditionally the dish was left baking all day.

MOROCCAN CHICKEN TAGINE

Metric	Ingredient	Imperial
1.4 kg	bone-in chicken pieces, skin removed	3 lbs
500 ml	chicken broth	2 cups
	1 can diced tomatoes, undrained	
	2 onions, chopped	
230 g	dried apricots, chopped	1 cup
	4 cloves garlic, minced	
10 g	ground cumin	2 tsp
5 g	ground cinnamon	1 tsp
5 g	ground ginger	1 tsp
2 g	ground coriander	1/2 tsp
2 g	ground red pepper	1/2 tsp
	6 sprigs fresh cilantro	
14 g	cornstarch	1 tbsp
14 g	water	1 tbsp
	1 can chickpeas (garbanzo beans), drained and rinsed	
30 g	chopped fresh cilantro	2 tbsp
60 g	slivered almonds, toasted	1/4 cup

Method

1. **Place the chicken in** a slow cooker. Combine the broth, tomatoes, onions, apricots, garlic, cumin, cinnamon, ginger, coriander, red pepper and cilantro in medium bowl then pour over the chicken. Cover and cook on low for 4 to 5 hours or until chicken is tender.

2. **Transfer the chicken to** a serving platter; cover to keep warm. Combine the cornstarch and water in small bowl until smooth. Stir cornstarch mixture and chickpeas into a slow cooker. Cover and cook on high for 15 minutes or until sauce is thickened.

3. **Pour sauce over chicken.** Sprinkle with cilantro and toasted almonds and serve with couscous.

PICKLED PARTRIDGE

Metric	Ingredient	Imperial	Metric	Ingredient	Imperial
	(for the pickled partridge pâté and jelly stock)			(for the lentil vinaigrette)	
			100 g	of cooked lentils	3 1/2 oz
	1 home-pickled partridge			modena vinegar	
	1 fresh celery			extra virgin olive oil	
	1 drizzle of extra virgin olive oil			salt	
	bay vinegar and pepper			(for the tempura)	
	pickled onion		500 ml	water	2 cups
	gelatin leaves		15 g	sea salt	3 tsp
100 g	double cream flavoured with spices	3 1/2 oz	15 g	salt	3 tsp
			15 g	sugar	3 tsp
			3 g	yeast	1/2 tsp

Method

1. **Remove the bones and** skin from the pickled partridge. To make the emulsion, crush the partridge meat with the traditional pickle ingredients (pickled onion, bay vinegar and pepper and 1 drizzle of olive oil).

2. **When you have obtained** the emulsion, mix it with the flavoured whipped cream at a ratio of 2 parts to one. Leave to stand for 20 hours in cold store.

3. **Make the pickle jelly** by adding 1/2 gelatin leaf for every 1/2 litre of pickle stock. Make traditional tempura, mixing the ingredients and sieving them. Mix the ingredients of the lentil vinaigrette.

4. **Clean the celery, cut** the stalks into small pieces and place them on the plate; set aside the leaves for frying in tempura. Place a partridge emulsion quenelle and the celery leaves in tempura on top of the celery salad. Pour the lentil vinaigrette made with Modena vinegar and the pickle jelly over the lot.

PORK RUMP IN RED WINE

Metric	Ingredient	Imperial
14 g	brown sugar	1 tbsp
14 g	red wine	1 tbsp
14 g	soy sauce	1 tbsp
14 g	cornflour	1 tbsp
5 g	oil	1 tsp
5 g	cinnamon	1 tsp
5 g	minced garlic	1 tsp
500 g	Trim Pork rump steaks, diced	1 lb
250 ml	plum sauce	1 cup
250 ml	red wine	1 cup

Method

1. **Mix the brown sugar,** red wine, soy sauce, cornflour, oil, cinnamon and garlic together in a bowl.

2. **Add the Trim pork,** toss, cover and leave in the refrigerator for about one hour.

3. **Preheat oven to 170°C.** Heat the sesame oil in a pan, remove pork from the marinade and add to the pan. Stir fry until brown. Transfer to a casserole dish.

4. **Add the reserved marinade,** plum sauce and red wine to the pan. Bring to the boil, then pour over the pork.

5. **Cover the casserole and** place in the preheated oven.

6. **Cook for 1 1/4** to 1 1/2 hours or until the pork is tender. Serve with wild rice and steamed vegetables.

POTATO, CARROT AND GREEN BEAN STEW

Metric	Ingredient	Imperial
	4 large carrots, thinly sliced	
	2 large potatoes, thinly sliced	
	1 large onion, thinly sliced	
450 g	green beans	1lb
	2 cloves garlic, smashed	
1.5 ml	chicken stock	6 cups
15 ml	olive oil	1 tbsp
2 g	dried thyme	1/4 tsp
2 g	dried basil	1/4 tsp
5 g	dried parsley	1 tsp
5 g	1 teaspoon salt	1 tsp
	ground black pepper to taste	

Method

1. **Combine the carrots, potatoes,** onion, green beans, garlic, chicken stock, olive oil, thyme, basil, parsley, salt, and pepper in a stock pot over medium-high heat.

2. **Bring to a simmer** and cook until the carrots are tender, for about 20 minutes. Transfer to a blender in small batches and blend until smooth.

RABBIT STEW

Metric	Ingredient	Imperial
1.3 kg	rabbit, diced	3 lb
	6 peeled, small white onions	
345 g	diced celery	1 1/2 cups
23 g	salt	4 1/2 tsp
1 g	pepper	1/8 tsp
1.8 litres	boiling water	2 qts
460 g	diced carrots	2 cups
460 g	diced potatoes	2 cups
115 g	flour	1/2 cup
190 ml	cold water	3/4 cup
14 g	chopped parsley	1 tbsp
	handful of green olives	

Method

1. **Wash and dry the** cleaned rabbit.

2. **Place in a large** pan with the onion, celery, salt, pepper, water, olives, and carrots.

3. **Cover and simmer 2** hours or until the rabbit is tender.

4. **Add the potatoes. Blend** the flour and water.

5. **Stir the flour mix** into the stew. Cook until thickened and add parsley to serve.

RATATOUILLE

Metric	Ingredient	Imperial
	Olive oil	
	1 onion	
	1 clove garlic, or to taste	
	1 eggplant (aubergine)	
	1 green, red, yellow or a combination, bell pepper	
	2 zucchini (courgettes) (cucumber also works well)	
	6 medium tomatoes, ripe (juicy), peeled and seeded	
	salt and pepper to taste	
	Herbes de Provence to taste	

Method

1. **Put a large casserole** dish on a medium heat. When the casserole dish is hot, add enough olive oil to just cover the bottom.

2. **Cut the zucchini and** eggplant into 1/2 inch slices. Then cut these into rectangles of about 3 by 1 inches. Add to the casserole. Sauté the slices until light brown

3. **Chop the onions and** garlic. Cut the green pepper into strips or dice, as preferred.

4. **Add the onions and** peppers and cook slowly for about 10 minutes until tender but not brown. Stir in the garlic.

5. **Peel and seed the** tomatoes. Dice them or cut them into quarters, add to the casserole. Five minutes later, check to see if the tomatoes have made enough juice to almost cover the vegetables - if so, perfect. If not, add water as needed.

6. **Add salt, pepper and** Herbes de Provence to taste. In general, 1 tsp of salt, 1/2 tsp of pepper and 1 tbsp of the herbs will suffice.

7. **Cover the casserole and** let simmer on low heat until the vegetables are tender but still intact, 10 to 20 minutes, or to taste.

8. **Remove the lid, raise** the heat a little and cook uncovered for another 15 minutes, basting frequently until the liquids have mostly evaporated, leaving a small amount of juice and olive oil.

ROAST GUINEA FOWL

Metric	Ingredient	Imperial
2 kg	guinea fowl	4 1/2 lb
	6 fresh rosemary sprigs	
	2 lemons, halved	
	4 garlic cloves	
	(for the sweet-and-sour gravy)	
50g	butter, at room temperature	1 1/2 oz
	olive oil	1 tbsp
500g	shallots, halved	2 cups
	leaves of 1 sprig fresh rosemary, finely chopped	
75ml	balsamic vinegar	1/4 cup
600ml	fresh chicken stock, hot	2 cups
14 g	plain flour	1 tbsp

Method

1. **Preheat the oven to** 190ºC/fan 170ºC/gas 5. Wash the guinea fowl and dry thoroughly with kitchen paper. Season inside and out. Put 3 rosemary sprigs inside each bird and place in a large roasting tin. Squeeze a lemon half over each bird, then stuff the squeezed half, along with an unsqueezed half and 2 garlic cloves, inside each cavity. Loosely cover the tin with foil.

2. **Roast in the oven** for 30 minutes, then remove the foil and roast for a further 20-30 minutes or until golden and cooked through. (To check if they are ready, insert a skewer into the thickest part of the thighs – the juices should run clear.) Transfer to a platter, cover loosely with foil and leave to rest.

3. **Meanwhile, make the gravy.** Heat half the butter and the olive oil in a medium saucepan over a low heat. Add the shallots. Cover and cook, stirring occasionally, for 30 minutes or until lightly golden. Remove the lid and cook for a further 15 minutes or until tender and caramelised. Stir in the rosemary and cook briefly, then add the vinegar – stand back, as it may splutter. Simmer vigorously until reduced and syrupy, then add the stock and simmer for a further 10 minutes or until reduced slightly. Mash together the remaining butter and the flour to make a beurre manié. Gradually whisk this into the sauce and simmer until thickened slightly. Season and keep warm.

4. **Transfer the birds to** a chopping board and remove the legs. Cut through the joint to separate into thighs and drumsticks, then remove the breasts in 1 piece and cut each into 3 pieces on the diagonal. Divide the meat between 6 plates, pour the gravy over the top and serve immediately with the Parsnip mash and Sautéed broccoli with garlic.

ROASTED PHEASANT WITH ORANGE

Metric	Ingredient	Imperial
	2 pheasants	
14 g	butter, melted	1 tbsp
	(apple-celery dressing)	
920 g	seasoned stuffing mix	4 cups
115 g	onion, chopped	1/2 cup
	1 egg, lightly beaten	
115 g	butter	1/2 cup
115 g	celery, chopped	1/2 cup
250 ml	boiling water	1 cup
230 g	apple, chopped	1 cup
	(orange gravy)	
30 g	cornstarch	2 tbsp
250 ml	orange juice	1 cup
60 g	brown sugar, firmly packed	1/4 cup
250 ml	chicken broth	1 cup
70 g	orange rind, julienned	1/3 cup
45 ml	dry white wine	3 tbsp
60 g	granulated sugar	1/4 cup

Method

1. **Prepare the stuffing and** spoon lightly into the pheasant cavities. Place the birds breast side up on a rack in roasting pan and brush with the melted butter. Roast covered for 2-3 hrs. at 325 F. or until internal temperature of stuffing reaches 165 F. Lard birds or baste frequently.

2. **Make the dressing. Toss** together the stuffing mix and the apple in a large bowl. Melt the butter in a small skillet then add the celery, and onion then stir frequently for 2-3 minutes until tender, then add to the stuffing mixture. Stir in the water and egg until well blended.

3. **For the gravy. Remove** pheasants and place them on a serving platter to keep warm. Drain drippings from roasting pan, leaving the brown particles in the pan and then sprinkle with cornstarch. Stir and cook over a medium heat until just blended, then remove from the heat. Gradually stir in the chicken broth, orange juice, orange rind, sugars, and wine. Return to the heat; stirring constantly, and bring to a boil. Boil for 1 minute.

ROASTED TURKEY

Metric	Ingredient	Imperial
	(for the stuffing mix)	
920 g	crumbled cornbread	4 cups
5 g	kosher salt	1 tsp
5 g	freshly ground black pepper	1 tsp
10 g	dried/rubbed sage	2 tsp
230 g	dried apples, diced	1 cup
170 g	walnuts, roughly chopped	3/4 cup
250 ml	buttermilk	1 cup
60 g	dried cherries, stemmed and finely chopped	1/4 cup
	8 egg yolks, beaten	
	1 stick butter, softened and whipped	
575 g	shredded cooked chicken or turkey	2 1/2 cups
	(for the turkey)	
	1 (18 pound) whole turkey	
115 g	butter, softened	1/2 cup
1.4 litres	turkey stock	1 1/2 quarts

Method

1. **Make the stuffing: Combine** the stuffing ingredients in a bowl and mix well. Place the stuffing in the turkey cavity and cook it along with the turkey. Make sure the stuffing reaches 165 degrees Fahrenheit before serving. If it doesn't, then scoop it out and bake it alone in the oven until it does.

2. **Preheat oven to 325** degrees Fahrenheit. Place the rack in the lowest position of the oven. Remove the neck and giblets. Rinse the turkey and pat it dry with paper towels. Place the turkey, breast side up, on a rack in the roasting pan. Rub the skin with softened butter, and season with salt and pepper.

3. **Fill the body cavity** with stuffing. Place a meat thermometer in the thickest part of one thigh. Position an aluminum foil tent over the turkey. Place the turkey in the oven, and pour two cups of turkey broth into the bottom of the roasting pan.

4. **Baste the entire turkey** every 30 minutes with the juices on the bottom of the pan. Add stock to the drippings as they become dry, about one to two cups at a time. Remove aluminum foil tent after two and a half hours.

5. **Roast until the meat** reaches 185 degrees Fahrenheit and the stuffing reaches 165 degrees Fahrenheit. This should take about 4 hours.

SLOW-COOKED APRICOT CHICKEN

Metric	Ingredient	Imperial
	6 frozen skinless, boneless chicken breasts (not thawed)	
	1 package dry onion soup mix	
125 ml	Russian or French salad dressing	1/2 cup
230 g	apricot preserves or jam	1 cup
30 g	apple cider vinegar	2 tbsp
5 g	dried thyme or basil leaves	1 tsp
1 g	pepper	1/8 tsp

Method

1. **In a 3-4 quart** slow cooker, arrange the chicken pieces.

2. **Mix the remaining ingredients** in a medium bowl and then pour over the chicken. Stir coat until the mixture coats the breats. Cover and cook on low for 6-8 hours until the chicken is thoroughly cooked and tender.

3. **If you like, you** can thicken the mixture before serving: Combine 2 tablespoons cornstarch with 3 tablespoons water or chicken stock and mix until smooth. Add to the cooker; turn to high for 10-15 minutes until sauce is thickened. Serve with hot cooked rice or pasta.

SPICY CAJUN CHICKEN WITH BEAN STEW

Metric	Ingredient	Imperial
	(for the chicken)	
	1 chicken breat flattened out to 3cm/1in	
50g	plain flour	1¾oz
	2 free-range eggs, beaten	
50g	breadcrumbs	1¾oz
2 g	chilli powder	½ tsp
2 g	cayenne powder	½tsp
45 ml	oil	3 tbsp
	(for the bean stew)	
30 ml	olive oil	2 tbsp
	½ red onion	
	1 garlic clove, chopped	
100g	haricot beans, tinned, rinsed and drained	3½oz
2 g	chilli powder	½ tsp
2 g	ground cumin powder	½tsp
200ml	chicken stock	7¼fl oz
	3 tomatoes	

Method

1. **Combine chicken and tomatoes** in large pot then bring to a boil.

2. **Cover; reduce heat and** simmer for 1 hour.

3. **Add remaining ingredients. Bring** to a boil. Reduce heat and simmer, uncovered, for 1 hour or until vegetables are tender, stirring occasionally.

STEAK AND KIDNEY PIE

Metric	Ingredient	Imperial
900 g	bottom round or chuck steak	2 lb
450 g	veal kidneys	1 lb
225 g	mushrooms	1/2 lb
60 g	flour	1/4 cup
	Butter or oil	
	Salt & freshly ground pepper	
340 g	onion, cut into 1/2" cubes	3/4 lb
2 g	minced garlic	1/2 tsp
1.5 litre	beef broth	6 cup
45 ml	Worcestershire sauce	3 tbsp
15 ml	Louisiana Red Hot Sauce (not Tabasco)	1 tbsp
14 g	tomato paste	1 tbsp
1 g	dried thyme	1/4 tsp
	Pie pastry	

Method

1. **Cut steak into 1"** to 1 1/2" squares. Trim away and discard the white tough core and sinews from the kidneys and cut into 1/2" cubes. Coat the steak and kidney separately with seasoned flour. Toss well and shake off any excess. Cut the mushrooms into quarters or slices.

2. **Heat the butter or** oil in a heavy skillet and lightly brown the steak. Remove, then brown the kidney. Place steak and kidney in warm dish.

3. **Saute the onion until** then add the mushrooms and garlic until the mushrooms start to brown. Remove to a 4 or 5 quart cooking pot over low medium heat and add tomato paste, Worcestershire sauce, hot sauce and thyme. Slowly add sufficient stock, stirring all the time, until it becomes a gravy. Add seasoned flour if needed. Bring to a boil and cook about 5 minutes.

4. **Season to taste and** place the steak and kidney in the cooking pot. Add additional stock so that the meat is almost covered. Cover with a lid and place in an oven at 300F and bake for about 1 1/2 hours or until the steak is thoroughly tender. Cool and refrigerate overnight.

5. **Spoon the meat and** sauce into an 8-cup baking pan (oval dish measuring 13"x8"x2" is ideal). The pie should have plenty of gravy and not become dry. Brush around the outside edge of the baking dish with a beaten egg. Cover with the pie pastry. Decorate with pastry cut outs. Cut a hole 1" or smaller in the center of the pastry and a few slashes to allow steam to escape. Brush with a little beaten egg. Set dish on a flat pan and place in oven. Bake at 425 F for 40 minutes.

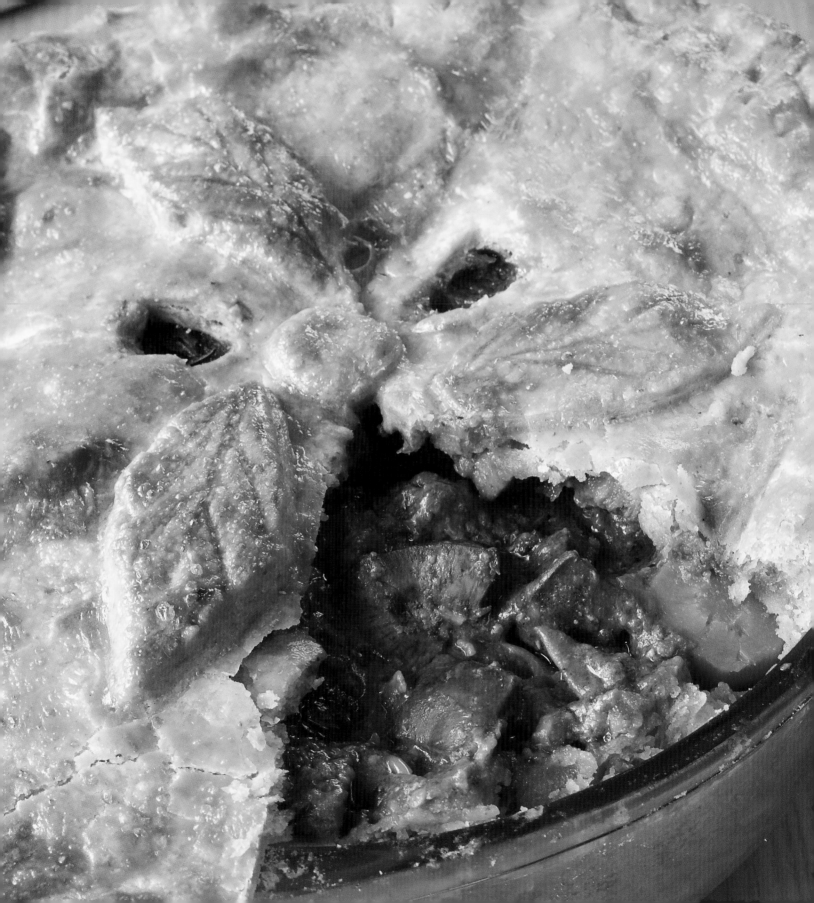

VENISON CASSEROLE

Metric	Ingredient	Imperial
500 g	buttery mashed potatoes	2 cups
450 g	lean ground venison (or other big game)	1 lb
15 ml	canola oil	1 tbsp
	1 red onion, chopped	
	2 cloves garlic, minced	
	2 stalks celery, diced	
115 g	diced red bell pepper	1/2 cup
15 ml	Worcestershire sauce	1 tbsp
2 g	salt	1/2 tsp
1 g	pepper	1/4 tsp
	2 eggs, beaten	
230 g	cottage cheese	1 cup
	2 tomatoes, sliced	
230 g	shredded Colby Jack or Cheddar cheese	1 cup

Method

1. **Preheat oven to 350** degrees F (175 degrees C).

2. **Spread mashed potatoes evenly** in a 2-quart casserole dish; set aside. Brown the venison in a large skillet over medium-high heat until crumbly and no longer pink, set aside.

3. **Heat the canola oil** in the skillet, then stir in the red onion, garlic, celery, and red bell pepper. Cook until the onion has softened, about 3 minutes. Stir in cooked venison, and season with Worcestershire, salt, and pepper. Spoon mixture onto potatoes in the casserole dish.

4. **Stir together eggs and** cottage cheese in a small bowl; spread evenly over meat mixture. Top with tomato slices, and sprinkle with cheese.

5. **Bake, uncovered, in preheated** oven until set, about 20 minutes.

WINTER GAME CASSEROLE

Metric	Ingredient	Imperial
50g	butter	1/4 cup
	2 sticks celery, finely sliced	
	16 shallots, peeled	
680g	Mixed Game Casserole (duck, pigeon, pheasant and partridge)	1 1/2 lb
250 ml	Organic Vintage Cider	1 cup
	4 sprigs fresh thyme	
	2 small English eating apples, such as Cox's, cut into wedges and cored	
100g	crème fraîche	1/2 cup

Method

1. **Preheat the oven to** 180ºC, gas mark 4. In an ovenproof casserole dish, melt a knob of the butter and fry the celery for 1-2 minutes until starting to soften. Using a slotted spoon, transfer the celery to a plate. Add the shallots to the pan and cook for 1-2 minutes until starting to brown. Remove and add to the celery.

2. **Add more butter to** the hot pan and fry half the game for about 2 minutes until lightly browned. Repeat with the remaining game.

3. **Return the celery, shallots** and game to the pan and stir to combine. Add the cider and allow to bubble for 1 minute. Add 2 of the thyme sprigs and season to taste. Put the lid on the casserole dish and cook in the oven for 40 minutes or until the game is tender.

4. **Heat a frying pan,** add the remaining butter and fry the apple for 2-3 minutes until it starts to caramelise and turn golden brown. Remove from the pan and keep warm on a plate covered with foil.

5. **Stir the crème fraîche** into the casserole and serve immediately, scattered with the apple and remaining thyme leaves. Serve with chunks of seeded wholemeal bread or mashed potato.

YORKSHIRE PUDDING FILLED WITH STEWED BEEF

Metric	Ingredient	Imperial
1 kg	steak	2 lb
	2 veal kidneys, cubed and trimmed	
60 g	flour	1/4 cup
60 ml	oil	4 tbsp
	1 medium onion, thinly sliced	
125 g	mushrooms, sliced	1/2 cup
250 ml	beef broth	1 cup
250 ml	dry red wine	1 cup
14 g	tomato paste	1 tbsp
5 ml	worcestershire sauce	1 tsp
2 g	salt	1/2 tsp
1 g	pepper	1/4 tsp
1 g	tarragon	1/4 tsp
1 g	rosemary	1/4 tsp
	2 carrots, diced	
	2 eggs	
250 ml	milk	1 cup
230 g	flour	1 cup
2 g	salt	1/2 tsp

Method

1. **Make the Yorkshire Pudding:** Beat 2 eggs in bowl. Mix in 1 cup of milk, sift in 1 cup of flour and 1/2 tsp salt. Beat until smooth. Allow to rest rest in the fridge while the stew is cooking.

2. **Make the Stew. Coat** steak and kidneys with flour. Brown several pieces at a time in oil in stock pot; remove. Sauté the onion in pan drippings until tender.

3. **Add the mushrooms. Cook** for several minutes longer. Stir in the broth, wine, tomato paste and next 5 seasonings and diced carrots. Return meat to the pan. Cover and cook on a slow simmer,for 2 hours or until tender (don't let stew dry out, add a little water if needed and reduce heat slightly). Preheat oven to 200°C.

4. **Heat 2 tbs oil** in a 6-8 cup casserole. Pour batter into hot casserole dish. Spoon stew over batter to within 1 inch of edge. Bake at 200c for 30 minutes or until puffed and brown.

CHOCOLATE CAKE

Metric	Ingredient	Imperial
400 g	all-purpose flour	1 3/4 cups
460 g	white sugar	2 cups
170 g	unsweetened cocoa powder	3/4 cup
10 g	baking soda	2 tsp
5 g	baking powder	1 tsp
5 g	salt	1 tsp
	2 eggs	
250 ml	strong brewed coffee	1 cup
250 ml	buttermilk	1 cup
125 ml	vegetable oil	1/2 cup
5 ml	vanilla extract	1 tsp

Method

1. **Preheat oven to 350** degrees F (175 degrees C). Grease and flour two 9 inch round cake pans or one 9x13 inch pan.

2. **In large bowl combine** flour, sugar, cocoa, baking soda, baking powder and salt. Make a well in the center.

3. **Add eggs, coffee, buttermilk,** oil and vanilla. Beat for 2 minutes on medium speed. Batter will be thin. Pour into prepared pans.

4. **Bake at 350 degrees** F (175 degrees C) for 30 to 40 minutes, or until toothpick inserted into center of cake comes out clean. Cool for 10 minutes, then remove from pans and finish cooling on a wire rack. Fill and frost as desired.

CREAMED RICE PUDDING

Metric	Ingredient	Imperial
170 g	uncooked white rice	3/4 cup
500 ml	milk, divided	2 cups
70 g	white sugar	1/3 cup
1 g	salt	1/4 tsp
	1 egg, beaten	
140 g	golden raisins	2/3 cup
14 g	butter	1 tbsp
3 ml	vanilla extract	1/2 tsp

Method

1. **In a medium saucepan,** bring 1 1/2 cups water to a boil. Add the rice and stir.

2. **Reduce the heat, cover** and simmer for 20 minutes.

3. **In another saucepan, combine** 1 1/2 of cups cooked rice, 1 1/2 cups of milk, sugar and salt. Cook over medium heat until thick and creamy, 15 to 20 minutes.

4. **Stir in the remaining** 1/2 cup of milk, beaten egg and raisins. Cook for 2 minutes more, stirring constantly.

5. **Remove from heat, and** stir in the butter and vanilla. Serve warm.

HOME MADE APPLE PIE

Metric	Ingredient	Imperial	Metric	Ingredient	Imperial
	(for the Pie Crust)		575 g	sugar, and additional for sprinkling	2½ cup
225g	plain flour	8 oz	60 g	flour	¼ cup
110g	margarine	4 oz	35 g	cornstarch	2½ tbsp
55g	lard	2 oz		cinnamon	
	pinch of salt			nutmeg	
30 ml	cold water	2 tbsp		(for the Pie Topping)	
	(for the Pie Filling)		28g	milk	1 oz
500g	apples, sliced	1 lb		cinnamon	
30 ml	lemon juice	2 tbsp		sugar	
1 oz	salted butter	28g			

Method

1. **Prepare the pie crust.** Rub flour, margarine, lard, and salt together until the mixture has the consistency of fine breadcrumbs. Add 2 tablespoons water to make a soft but firm dough. Roll pastry on floured surface to the size you want your pie. Make two crusts. Place one crust in pie pan.

2. **Prepare the filling. Peel** and slice apples into 1/8th-1/4th inch thick segments. Add lemon juice to apples. Mix apples by hand with 1/2 cup sugar and a few dashes of cinnamon.

3. **Transfer the segments, minus** their acquired juices, to pie pan. Mix the rest of the sugar, cinnamon, nutmeg, flour, and cornstarch in a separate bowl. Pour this over the apples in pie pan then dot with butter.

4. **Cover with the other** crust. Firm down edges with fork or finger. Cut heart or diamond-shaped vents into top crust. **Brush the pastry top with** milk and sprinkle additional sugar and cinnamon over the top.

5. **Bake at 350 °F** (177 °C) until golden brown (about 60 minutes). Serve warm with ice cream or custard.

HOT BAKED APPLE WITH CINNAMON STICKS

Metric	Ingredient	Imperial
	10 apples, cored, peeled and sliced thin	
10 g	cinnamon	2 tsp
230 g	brown sugar	1 cup
10 ml	lemon juice	2 tsp
	1 dash salt	
	1 dash nutmeg	

Method

1. **Place the cut and peeled** apples in a mixing bowl and gently mix all of the ingredients together.

2. **Put the apples in a** non-stick pan, and cook them covered for 45 minutes at 375 degrees.

3. **Stir at least once every** 15 minutes.

4. **Once they are soft, cook** them for another few minutes to thicken the cinnamon sauce.

YULE LOG

Metric	Ingredient	Imperial	Metric	Ingredient	Imperial
	5 eggs, room temperature, separated		2 ml	vanilla extract	1/2 tsp
140 g	sugar	2/3 cup	115 g	chopped walnuts	1/2 cup
30 g	all-purpose flour	2 tbsp		(for the cream frosting)	
45 g	unsweetened cocoa	3 tbsp	230 g	butter, softened	1 cup
	(for the filling)		115 g	confectioners' sugar	1/2 cup
35 g	all-purpose flour	2 1/2 tbsp	14 g	unsweetened cocoa	1 tbsp
125 ml	milk	1/2 cup	5 g	strong coffee	1 tsp
115 ml	sugar	1/2 cup		chopped nuts	
125 ml	butter, softened	1/2 cup			

Method

1. **In a large mixing** bowl, beat the egg yolks at high speed until light and fluffy. Gradually add sugar, beating until mixture is thick and light-colored.

2. **Add flour and cocoa,** beating on a low speed. In another bowl, beat the egg whites until soft peaks form; fold into batter. mix until no streaks of white are remaining.

3. **Grease a 15-in. x** 10-in. x 1-in. pan; line with waxed paper, and grease and flour the paper. Spread the batter evenly in the pan. Bake at 350 degrees F for 15 minutes or until cake springs back when touched lightly.

4. **Cover with waxed paper** and cool completely on the wire rack then remove the paper; invert cake onto an 18-in. long piece of waxed paper dusted with confectioners' sugar.Trim edges from all four sides of cake.

5. **For the filling, combine** the flour and milk in a saucepan. Cook over low heat; stirring until thick then allow to cool. In a mixing bowl, cream the sugar, butter and vanilla. Add the flour mixture; beat until fluffy.

6. **Fold in walnuts if** desired. Spread the mixture onto cake; roll up, jelly-roll style, starting from one short end. For frosting, beat butter until fluffy in a small bowl. Beat in sugar, cocoa and coffee. Spread over the cake, using a fork to create a bark-like effect. Sprinkle with confectioners' sugar and nuts if desired.